11/10

S0-ASL-902

--LYNNFIELD PUBLIC LIBRARY--
LYNNFIELD, MA 01940

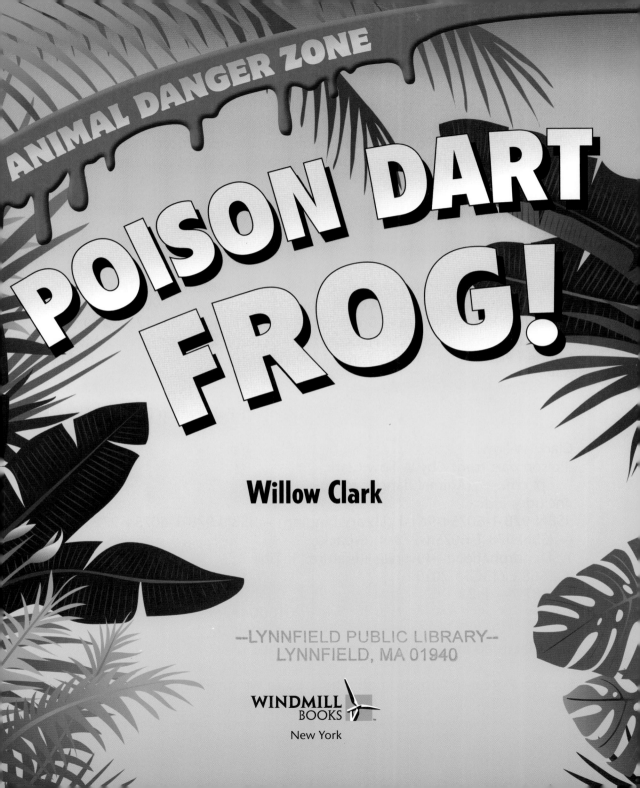

ANIMAL DANGER ZONE

POISON DART FROG!

Willow Clark

--LYNNFIELD PUBLIC LIBRARY--
LYNNFIELD, MA 01940

WINDMILL
BOOKS

New York

Published in 2011 by Windmill Books, LLC
303 Park Avenue South, Suite # 1280, New York, NY 10010-3657

Copyright © 2011 by Windmill Books, LLC

All rights reserved. No part of this book may be reproduced in any form without permission in writing from the publisher, except by a reviewer.

CREDITS:
Author: Willow Clark
Edited by: Jennifer Way
Designed by: Brian Garvey

Photo Credits: Cover, pp. 4, 5, 6, 7, 8, 10, 11, 14 (bottom), 15, 16 (top), 18, 19, 22 (bottom) Shutterstock.com; Cover (background) © www.iStockphoto.com/Shannon Keegan; p. 9 Brent Stirton/Getty Images; pp. 12, 13, 20 © www.iStockphoto.com/Lee Hancock; pp. 14 (top), 22 (top) © Mark Moffett/Minden Pictures; pp. 16 (bottom), 17 © WILDLIFE/Peter Arnold Inc.; p. 21 AFP/Getty Images.

Library of Congress Cataloging-in-Publication Data

Clark, Willow.
 Poison dart frog! / by Willow Clark.
     p. cm. — (Animal danger zone)
 Includes index.
 ISBN 978-1-60754-961-1 (library binding) — ISBN 978-1-60754-972-7 (pbk.) — ISBN 978-1-60754-973-4 (6-pack)
 1. Dendrobatidae—Juvenile literature. I. Title.
 QL668.E233C53 2010
 597.87′7—dc22

                                        2010004426

Manufactured in the United States of America

For more great fiction and nonfiction, go to windmillbooks.com.

CPSIA Compliance Information: Batch #S10W: For further information contact Windmill Books, New York, New York at 1-866-478-0556.

TABLE OF CONTENTS

Small but Deadly

Poison dart frogs are small frogs that live in Central America and South America. Many are only about 1 inch (2.5 cm) long and weigh less than one ounce (28 g).

Poison dart frogs are very small. Here are some adult poison dart frogs sitting in a person's hand!

Poison dart frogs got their name because their skin has a deadly **poison**. This poison means that animals that eat other small frogs will steer clear of poison dart frogs!

There are more than 100 different kinds of poison dart frog. Poison dart frogs come in bright colors, such as yellow, blue, orange, and red.

These bright colors are not just for show. The poison dart frog's colorful skin sends a message to other animals. That message is, "Stay away from me. I'm poisonous!"

Poison dart frogs are **amphibians**. Amphibians spend the first part of their life in water and breathe using **gills**. Amphibians live their adult lives on land and breathe using **lungs**.

Salamanders are amphibians, too.

Amphibians stay close to ponds, lakes, and rivers so that their skin does not dry out. Poison dart frogs live in the plants and trees near a water source.

Adult poison dart frogs live on land but they stay near water. Like other frogs, they have soft skin that can dry out if they are away from water for too long.

Sticky pads

The poison dart frog has sticky pads on its toes. These pads help the frog to keep its footing as it moves around.

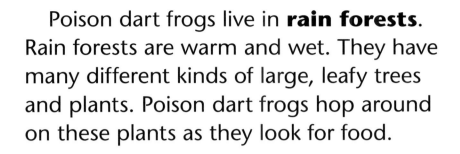

Poison dart frogs live in **rain forests**. Rain forests are warm and wet. They have many different kinds of large, leafy trees and plants. Poison dart frogs hop around on these plants as they look for food.

Poison dart frogs have sticky pads on the undersides of their toes. Those sticky pads keep this harlequin poison dart frog from sliding off the leaf.

You Are What You Eat

Poison dart frogs eat bugs such as ants, termites, crickets, fruit flies, and beetles. When the frog sees a bug, it flicks out its tongue to catch it. This happens very fast. Blink and you will miss it!

Poison dart frogs have a long, sticky tongue. They use this tongue to catch their food.

Poison dart frogs can climb onto leaves to hunt for bugs. With a flick of the tongue, it catches its meal.

Some native South Americans use the frog's poison on the tip of their darts.

It is thought that the bugs poison dart frogs eat make its skin poisonous. The poisons from the bugs build up in the frog's body but do not harm the frog.

Poison dart frogs that are raised in zoos are not poisonous. That is because when they live in zoos they have a different diet. They are not fed the bugs that they eat in the wild.

Poison dart frogs eat ants.

In the wild, poison dart frogs **mate** during the rainy season. The male frog attracts a female with his song. This "song" is a bunch of buzzing and trilling sounds.

The female poison dart frog lays eggs and then leaves. The male stays behind. He will guard the eggs and keep them moist until they hatch.

This male poison dart frog is guarding these eggs.

From Tadpole to Frog

When the eggs hatch, tadpoles, or baby frogs, wiggle out. The male frog takes the tadpoles onto his back and carries them to a pool of water. The tadpoles are now on their own.

Tadpoles live in the water until they have grown into frogs. As the tadpoles get bigger they grow legs, develop lungs, and lose their tail. The process of change is called **metamorphosis**.

Here is a male poison dart frog carrying tadpoles on his back. The tadpoles will be fully grown frogs in about 12 weeks.

Some kinds of poison dart frogs are **endangered**. This means that there are fewer of them than there used to be. They are in danger of dying out completely and being gone from the Earth forever.

The golden poison dart frog is endangered. They live in a small area of rain forest in Colombia, a country in South America.

This rain forest was burned to clear the land for farms and homes. Clearing rain forests leaves poison dart frogs with no place to live.

One reason some poison dart frogs are endangered is that the rain forests in which they live have been cut down to build farms and houses. This leaves the frogs with nowhere to live or find food.

Did You Know?

Poison dart frogs are also known as poison arrow frogs.

Poison dart frogs live for about three years in the wild. They can live for as long as ten years in zoos.

The golden poison dart frog has enough poison in its skin to kill 20,000 mice!

A group of frogs is called an army.

Frogs are just one kind of amphibian. Toads, salamanders, and newts are also amphibians.

GLOSSARY

amphibians (am-FIH-bee-unz) Animals that spend the first part of their life in water and the rest on land.

endangered (in-DAYN-jerd) In danger of no longer living.

gills (GILZ) Body parts that tadpoles use for breathing.

lungs (LUNGZ) The parts of an air-breathing animal that take in air.

mate (MAYT) To come together to make babies.

metamorphosis (meh-tuh-MOR-fuh-sus) A complete change in form.

poison (POY-zun) To cause pain or death with matter made by an animal's body.

rain forests (RAYN FOR-ests) Thick forests that get a lot of rain during the year.

INDEX

READ MORE

Bredeson, Carmen. *Poison Dart Frogs Up Close*. New York: Enslow Publishers, 2008.

Dussling, Jennifer. *Deadly Poison Dart Frogs*. New York: Bearport Publishing, 2008.

Wechsler, Doug. *Poison Dart Frogs*. New York: Rosen Publishing Group, 2005.

WEB SITES

For Web resources related to the subject of this book, go to: www.windmillbooks.com/weblinks and select this book's title.